Ally & Jordi's
Adventures Through Florida

FLORIDA DEPARTMENT *of* STATE

Book layout and design by Stephen B. Smith
Project coordination by Mark R. Ard

Source list available at AllyandJordisAdventures.com.

All images from the State Archives of Florida, Florida Memory,
unless otherwise noted.

All proceeds from the sale of this book benefit the Friends of the
Museums of Florida History, Inc., which supports the promotion
of Florida's history and culture for future generations.

Printed and bound by Rose Printing, Tallahassee, Florida.

ISBN 978-1-4675-7968-1

9 781467 579681

Ally & Jordi's
Adventures Through Florida

Presented by
First Lady Ann Scott

Written by Rachel Basan Porter
Illustrated by Sarah Shaw

Greetings From Florida's First Family

From the Desk of the First Lady

Governor Scott and I are so excited that you're joining Ally and Jordi on an adventure through the great state of Florida! Ally and Jordi are courageous girls who enjoy exploring Florida. You'll have the opportunity to join them as they learn about Florida's environment, history, pioneers and so much more!

On your adventure with Ally and Jordi, you'll see that our great state offers so many opportunities for adventure. I hope that you will visit each of Florida's 67 counties to experience the diverse cultures, foods, parks and attractions and find out what makes each place special. Pretty soon, you'll see for yourself why Governor Scott and I say that Florida truly is the best place to live, work and raise a family!

First Lady

Ann Scott

Ann Scott
First Lady of Florida

Pages 13-17

OUR STATE

Florida is known as "The Sunshine State." Discover more about what makes Florida unique.

NATURE

With more than 1,000 miles of coastline and lots of natural springs, Florida's environment is a treasure.

We'll explore more of Florida's natural wonders throughout our journey.

We live right here in Florida, and love exploring and learning about our home state. There is so much to see and do here! We are excited to share it all with you in this book.

Take a look at the map on the right. Pick the area of Florida you would like to visit, then turn to those pages and we will take you on a wonderful adventure through our amazing state.

So, go ahead! Choose where you want to visit, and let's go!

Look out for the "find it" pictures in this book – see if you can find all of the interesting facts about Florida!

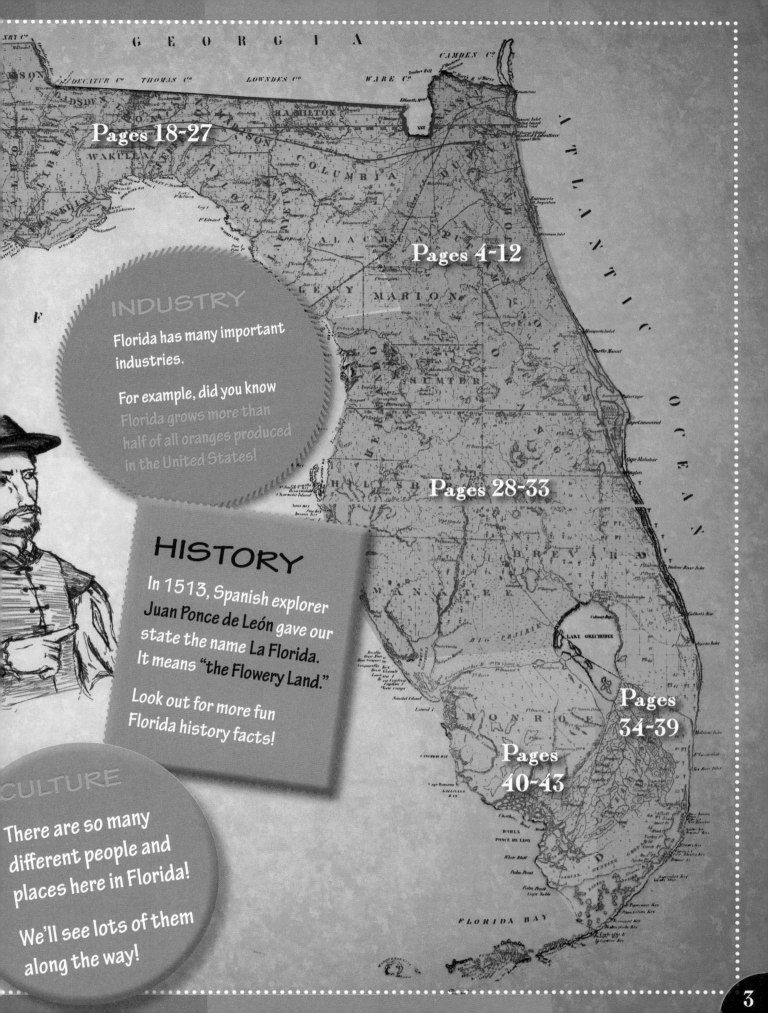

INDUSTRY

Florida has many important industries.

For example, did you know Florida grows more than half of all oranges produced in the United States!

HISTORY

In 1513, Spanish explorer Juan Ponce de León gave our state the name La Florida. It means "the Flowery Land."

Look out for more fun Florida history facts!

CULTURE

There are so many different people and places here in Florida!

We'll see lots of them along the way!

St. Augustine:
450 years and counting.

Modern history of Florida began in 1513, when European explorer Juan Ponce de León landed on Florida's east coast. In early April 1513, he claimed the land for Spain and gave it the name *"La Florida."*

Then in 1565, another Spanish explorer named Pedro Menéndez settled St. Augustine. Menéndez became the first Spanish governor of Florida.

Pedro Menéndez

Let's find out some more!

Fort Mose

The first official free black settlement in the United States was built here in Florida in 1738. It was called Fort Mose and it sat two miles north of St. Augustine. Captain Francisco Menendez was Fort Mose's black leader. Fort Mose was destroyed during an invasion from the English in 1740, then rebuilt in 1752. When Spain gave Florida to Britain in 1763, the families of Fort Mose fled to Cuba.

Castillo de San Marcos

This coquina fort in St. Augustine is the oldest masonry fort in the United States. Construction on Castillo de San Marcos started in 1672, but there were earlier wooden forts that protected the people of St. Augustine as well as Spanish treasure fleets sailing back to Spain.

Today, Castillo de San Marcos is a National Monument that is cared for by the National Park Service.

Photo courtesy of Glen Hastings

Nature

Coquina is formed from layers of crushed shells, cemented together over thousands of years.

The St. Augustine Lighthouse was built in 1874. Wooden and then coquina watchtowers served as the lighthouse before the black and white striped brick tower seen today. There are 219 steps on the iron staircase leading to the top. It is one of the few lighthouses in the United States with a working Fresnel lens. They even say that the lighthouse is haunted!

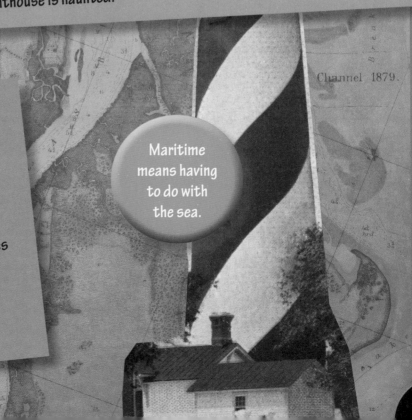

SAILING DIRECTIONS

Channel 1879.

Seafaring and Boat Building

From cruise ships to oyster skiffs, Florida industries were built upon our rich maritime heritage. Florida is surrounded by water on three sides, and our maritime heritage dates back to thousands of years before the Spanish arrived. Native Americans hollowed out huge cypress trees to make canoes. Spanish explorers then arrived on large sailing ships, called *Galleons*. Many different boats move through Florida's lakes, rivers and springs.

Maritime means having to do with the sea.

St. Augustine

"Way down upon the Swanee..."

Ray Charles

St. Augustine was once home to Florida Artists Hall of Fame musician Ray Charles, who attended the Florida School for the Deaf and Blind. Ray Charles was born in Georgia but lived here in Florida for many years. He even adapted Florida's official state song, "Old Folks at Home," to the hit song "Swanee River Rock."

Oldest School House

Along one of the oldest streets in St. Augustine is a wooden one-room schoolhouse that is more than 300 years old! The children of St. Augustine learned in this small building that is today held down by a giant anchor so that a hurricane won't blow it away!

Tourism

In the late 1800s, Henry Flagler and his friend Henry Plant thought if they built railroads and fancy hotel resorts then more visitors would come to Florida. Flagler's railroad helped connect cold northern states like New York to the tropical paradise of Key West. The railway made new towns, homes and jobs for people who moved there.

Henry Flagler

Thanks to the efforts of the two Henrys, Florida now welcomes more than 100 million tourists every year and more than 1 million people work in tourism.

Henry Flagler's train car

Photo courtesy of ACCORD and Frank Murray

(L-R) Andrew Young, Martin Luther King Jr., and Dr. Robert Hayling at a press conference in St. Augustine, 1964

The Andrew Young Crossing located in St. Augustine's central *Plaza de la Constitucion* monumentalizes the four core values of the Civil Rights movement: Freedom, Non-violence, Equality and Justice.

ANDREW YOUNG CROSSING

ANDREW YOUNG CROSSING

Jacksonville

Jacksonville is a really big city! It is almost 850 square miles, which makes it the largest city in the continental United States! Jacksonville is also the most populous city in Florida.

Who knew?!

Fort Caroline on the St. Johns River in modern-day Jacksonville was built in 1564. It was once home to more than 300 French settlers! The French explorer, Jean Ribault, led expeditions to create this French colony in the New World.

The French rule over Florida ended in 1565 when Pedro Menéndez arrived, settled St. Augustine and took Fort Caroline. Very few of the French escaped when the fort was destroyed by Menéndez. Today, you can visit the Fort Caroline monument and museum that recreates the original French settlement.

The Native Americans

who met French settlers were called the Timucua (Tee-MOO-qua). It is estimated that there were between 50,000 and 200,000 Timucua who lived in villages that spanned from what is now southern Georgia to the Orlando area.

The Cummer Museum of Art and Gardens sits on the banks of the St. Johns River. The building houses thousands of art masterpieces, while the tranquil surroundings boast artfully sculpted gardens. A visit wouldn't be complete without a stroll through the Italian garden and a photo op next to the marble fountain.

NATURE

The St. Johns River is 310 miles long. It flows from south to north! So, when you're in Jacksonville – in the north of Florida – you will see the end of Florida's longest river.

Photo courtesy of Jonathan Zander

Ocala

The countryside around Ocala is full of beautiful horses, farms and ranches. There is the amazing Ocala National Forest and lots of crystal clear springs. This rural setting is an important part of Florida's agriculture industry. Farm animals graze on the rolling pastures, while the forests are home to wild animals.

Cattle and horses that now occupy our grasslands roamed freely when they were first brought to Florida by the Spanish in the 1500s.

"Cow hunters" would ride through the forests to find their cattle. Those hunters have been called "cracker cowboys," perhaps because the sound of their bull whip made a mighty crack. Historic cattle drives like The Great Florida Cattle Drive, which herds 500 cattle across Florida, still take place and share the heritage of the "Florida Crackers."

There are 17.3 million acres of forest lands in Florida.

Zora Neale Hurston

African-American folklorist Zora Neale Hurston (1891 - 1960) was the daughter of former slaves who moved to Florida as a child. She documented many cultures, including the stories, songs and way of life for people working in Florida turpentine camps. The camps were deep in the forests where the workers collected pine sap to make turpentine. Zora also lived and worked in New York and is recognized for her work in the Harlem Renaissance. Zora worked in many different places where she learned and wrote about how people there lived. In addition to recording hundreds of songs and stories, Zora wrote several books, articles and theatrical plays.

Springs

Florida has more than 900 freshwater springs. Some of the largest and most popular include Silver Springs and Weeki Wachee. The springs stay at a constant temperature around 70 degrees – perfect for our state marine mammal, and one of our favorites, the manatee.

Some of Florida's springs preserve evidence of the first Floridians from 14,550 years ago.

Are Mermaids Real?

They say that in Florida, dreams come true. Well, our dream of seeing mermaids came true at Weeki Wachee Springs! At this unique aquarium-like attraction, mermaids perform for an audience seated in an underwater theatre. Mermaid shows began in the 1950s and continue today at this incredible Florida state park.

Florida's First Theme Park!

In the 1870s, as Florida was beginning to attract tourists, Hullam Jones and Philip Morell developed a boat with a glass bottom. Tourists would ride along Silver River and into Silver Springs. The glass bottom allowed them to see the natural underwater activity. Silver Springs may have been Florida's first theme park!

Adventurer Snack Recipes

Our adventures sometimes make us a little hungry. So we make easy snacks to keep us healthy and energized! You can make these snacks too.

Refrigerator Oatmeal

This is a tasty snack you make ahead. You'll need:

6 ounce carton of plain Greek yogurt
2/3 cup old fashioned rolled oats (not instant)
1/3 cup milk
Fresh Florida starfruit or mango – sliced (ask for help)
2 tablespoons honey
2 - ½ pint mason jars with lids

In a medium bowl, stir together yogurt, oats, milk, fruit and honey. Pour half of this mixture into each of the jars; cover tightly with the lid and put in the fridge overnight, up to 2 days. Enjoy!

Fruity Pizza

This is a fun twist on a tasty treat! You'll need:

1 whole wheat pita bread round
1 Florida Orange – peeled and sectioned
1/4 cup fresh Florida strawberries – sliced (ask for help)
1/4 cup blueberries
1 ounce cream cheese

Spread the cream cheese on top of your pita bread. Decorate your pizza with fresh fruit by creating a face or pattern – create your fun design!

Pensacola

Pensacola is the western-most city in the state of Florida. It is on the Gulf of Mexico coast and is named after the native Panzacola peoples who once lived here. Pensacola is one of Florida's most historic cities!

In 2009, Pensacola celebrated their 450th founding anniversary!

SHIPWRECK!

We discovered legendary ships and artificial reefs during our underwater explorations in Pensacola! Some of Florida's most famous colonial period shipwrecks lie at the bottom of Pensacola Bay. These remains are from Tristán de Luna's colony attempt of 1559. They sank during a hurricane on the evening of September 19, 1559. Also, the world's largest artificial reef is in Pensacola's waters – today skilled divers can experience the USS Oriskany and see the wildlife that live on this WWII-era former aircraft carrier.

Photo courtesy of Barry Shively

Photo courtesy of Visit Pensacola

The Blue Angels

First we saw the bright blue flash, then four colorful streaks painted the sky as the airplanes roared overhead. It was the world famous Blue Angels flying squadron! This special U.S. Naval Aviation team was formed by Admiral Chester Nimitz at Naval Air Station Jacksonville in the late 1940s. Their daredevil flying and endurance techniques helped advance the space program. Today, they perform to amazed crowds worldwide.

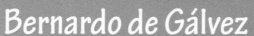

Bernardo de Gálvez

Many people think that the American Revolution was fought only in the North, but the courageous actions of this Spanish Governor of Louisiana helped lead to U.S. independence. During one of the longest battles of the war, Bernardo de Gálvez attacked British strongholds in West Florida and brought the U.S. troops essential supplies. Partly because of Bernardo de Gálvez, the British surrendered Pensacola and West Florida to Spain in May 1781.

Jacqueline Cochran and the WASPs

Northwest Florida native Jacqueline Cochran (left) formed the pioneering civilian all-female pilot organization known as the Women's Airforce Service Pilots, or WASPs. During World War II, the WASPs flew military aircraft for the U.S. Army. Their courage and duty paved the way for women's rights in the military.

Photo courtesy of San Diego Air and Space Museum

Photo courtesy of USGOV-PD

Fort Pickens

In the 1800s, the U.S. Army built forts on Pensacola's barrier islands to help protect the mainland. Fort Pickens was the largest and it is still standing today. With cool brick arches and 10 tall gun emplacements, this fort sits on the crystal white sands of the Gulf Islands National Seashore Park.

Destin

This Emerald Coast city is an underwater explorer's dream come true! Destin is popular for sports fishing and snorkeling because of the abundant sea life found in this area of the Gulf of Mexico. The white sparkling sands and emerald green water make Destin's natural treasure a real jewel.

Photo courtesy of State of Florida

Get Out and Play!

From parasailing and paddle boarding to fishing and snorkeling, the Emerald Coast is a fun place to learn a new watersport! On hot Florida summer days, visitors and residents can be spotted enjoying all the activities that this corner of paradise provides.

Beaches

The beaches in Destin were formed over 18,000 years ago at the end of the last Ice Age. Because much of the earth's water was frozen back then, the sea level of Florida was at least 100 miles further out to sea than it is now! When the ice melted, water flowed down through the mountains and into the rivers that opened to the Gulf of Mexico. The flow of water left tiny particles of powder-white quartz that make up Destin's beaches today.

Find These Words

Circle the letters in the puzzle below that spell these words.

A	A	Y	Q	F	E	E	R	W	N	I	C
P	D	V	M	T	E	U	R	N	O	C	H
A	P	E	N	S	A	C	O	L	A	N	Y
L	F	E	B	E	A	C	H	E	S	I	A
A	A	V	I	A	T	I	O	N	L	T	F
C	S	I	D	N	Z	O	F	C	P	S	X
H	O	X	Y	B	M	Y	B	H	X	E	P
I	I	Y	K	A	L	D	I	D	F	D	G
C	D	K	P	A	N	Z	A	C	O	L	A
O	P	L	K	C	E	R	W	P	I	H	S
L	R	E	T	A	W	N	E	Y	X	I	D
A	D	Y	Z	T	R	A	U	Q	G	U	M

BEACHES
PANZACOLA
AVIATION
WATER
REEF
DESTIN
APALACHICOLA
QUARTZ
SHIPWRECK
PENSACOLA

Make Jordi's Kite

For instructions on how to make Jordi's kite, visit AllyandJordisAdventures.com.

Apalachicola

This city was founded in the 1800s as an important port that connected the Gulf of Mexico to northern states through the Apalachicola River, allowing the delivery of cotton around the country. Also known for its world-famous oysters, this picturesque city is now a laid-back vacation spot!

Gulf coast seafood from Apalachicola helped put this city on the culinary map. In the early days, fishing was a big part of the Apalachicola economy because of the seafood trade. Today, people keep coming back to enjoy the delicious seafood and to fish from charter boats that take them to great fishing spots.

Air Conditioning

Apalachicola is well-known partly because of Dr. John Gorrie, who invented a way to cool air inside houses. Gorrie's device is considered the forerunner of modern-day air conditioning. Dr. Gorrie is remembered as one of Florida's most influential people and his statue is in the National Statuary Hall in Washington, D.C.

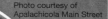

Cotton

The city of Apalachicola was the third largest cotton trading port on the Gulf of Mexico in the 1830s. Cotton was the reason the city boomed. There are still many historic buildings from that time. This one was the old cotton exchange.

Our State

Since November 18, 1883, Florida has had two time zones – Central and Eastern. The dividing line in our state follows the Apalachicola River from the Georgia border, but near the coast it veers west to include Port St. Joe. One famous legend says that was because of millionaire paper mill owner Ed Ball. Mr. Ball was very influential in Florida and he wanted his companies in Jacksonville and Port St. Joe to be in the same time zone! Maybe time really is money!

Ed Ball

19

Tallahassee

N ot everyone knows that Tallahassee has been Florida's capital since 1824. We found that out and more when we explored some of Florida's oldest sites in Tallahassee!

Before Florida was part of the USA, it had two capitals – St. Augustine and Pensacola. In 1822, a legislator was lost at sea while headed to a meeting in Pensacola. Territorial Governor William Pope Duval wanted to make things easier by designating just one capital, so he sent out one person on horseback from Jacksonville, and one person by boat from Pensacola until they met in the middle. So the old Native American town known as Tallahassee was established as Florida's capital city.

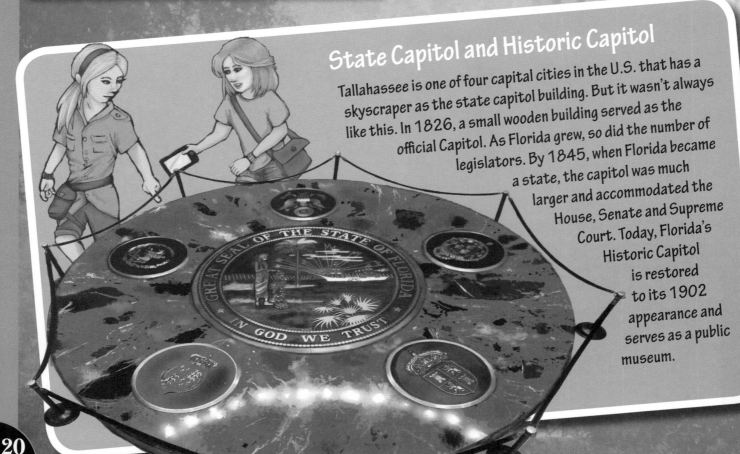

State Capitol and Historic Capitol

Tallahassee is one of four capital cities in the U.S. that has a skyscraper as the state capitol building. But it wasn't always like this. In 1826, a small wooden building served as the official Capitol. As Florida grew, so did the number of legislators. By 1845, when Florida became a state, the capitol was much larger and accommodated the House, Senate and Supreme Court. Today, Florida's Historic Capitol is restored to its 1902 appearance and serves as a public museum.

Governor's Mansion

A gracious home with quiet beauty

The People's House of Florida is also known as the Governor's Mansion. It is both the private residence of Florida's Governor and family and a public museum that we visited. It was first built in 1907, then rebuilt in 1956. Residents have updated the interior of this beautiful home several times. The most recent renovation restored its original 1950s style and charm. We love this place, especially the Florida Room and the Manatee Dance fountain in the gardens!

Photo courtesy of State of Florida

We the People

When Florida became the 27th state in the union on March 3, 1845, our founding principles were written down in the state constitution. Article 1 of Florida's constitution lays out the Declaration of Rights, which is the foundation of our freedoms and basic rights.

The Florida Constitution puts the power of government in the hands of the people and identifies three branches of government — legislative, executive and judicial. The legislative branch includes members of the Florida House and Senate, known as legislators; the executive branch includes Florida's Governor; and the judicial branch includes all of Florida's judges. The people of Florida choose their legislators and the leaders of the executive branch through elections. The three branches of government work together to make sure all Floridians' voices are heard.

How a Bill Becomes Law

If you have an idea for a law, you should talk to your district legislator. They could propose a bill. Bills can eventually become laws. But first they are discussed in the Florida House and Senate during a series of meetings held in the state capitol building called the legislative session. When everyone agrees what the bill should say they present it to the Governor, who will either sign it into law, veto it or leave it to become law on the effective date written into the bill. Veto means "I forbid" in Latin.

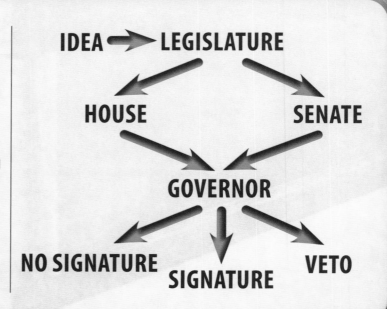

IDEA → LEGISLATURE

HOUSE   SENATE

GOVERNOR

NO SIGNATURE   SIGNATURE   VETO

Find These Words

Circle the letters in the puzzle below that spell these words.

```
U   C   D   V   L   V   S   Y   N   X
R   R   Z   O   E   K   B   J   K   E
H   T   Y   L   G   Z   O   A   G   E
E   L   E   R   I   E   Y   F   Y   S
A   O   E   Q   S   D   R   D   E   S
N   T   H   H   L   D   G   K   E   A
H   I   C   O   A   Q   U   H   E   H
A   P   A   T   T   E   P   V   T   A
I   A   L   O   O   T   V   S   A   L
C   C   A   S   R   T   D   S   N   L
A   J   P   E   J   S   J   Z   A   A
P   E   A   D   A   K   L   W   M   T
```

DESOTO
MANATEE
CAPITOL
DUVAL
ANHAICA
TALLAHASSEE
APALACHEE
LEGISLATOR

Florida Governors

Andrew Jackson
William Pope Duval
John Henry Eaton
Richard Keith Call
Robert Raymond Reid
Richard Keith Call
John Branch
William Dunn Moseley
Thomas Brown
James Emilius Broome
Madison Starke Perry
John Milton
Abraham Kurkindolle Allison

William Marvin
David Shelby Walker
Harrison Reed
Ossian Bingley Hart
Marcellus Lovejoy Stearns
George Franklin Drew
William Dunnington Bloxham
Edward Aylsworth Perry
Francis Philip Fleming
Henry Laurens Mitchell
William Dunnington Bloxham
William Sherman Jennings
Napoleon Bonaparte Broward

Albert Waller Gilchrist
Park Trammell
Sidney Johnston Catts
Cary Augustus Hardee
John Wellborn Martin
Doyle Elam Carlton
David Sholtz
Frederick Preston Cone
Spessard Lindsey Holland
Millard Fillmore Caldwell
Fuller Warren
Daniel Thomas McCarty
Charley Eugene Johns

Thomas "LeRoy" Collins
Cecil "Farris" Bryant
William "Haydon" Burns
Claude Roy Kirk, Jr.
Reubin O'Donovan Askew
Daniel Robert "Bob" Graham
John "Wayne" Mixson
Robert "Bob" Martinez
Lawton Mainor Chiles, Jr.
Kenneth Hood "Buddy" MacKay, Jr.
John Ellis "Jeb" Bush
Charles Joseph "Charlie" Crist
Richard L. "Rick" Scott

De Soto and the First Christmas

In 1539, several hundred Spanish explorers led by Hernando de Soto travelled through Florida on foot and horseback, and recorded early European interactions with Native Americans. Their writings describe a place named Anhaica, where they spent the winter of 1539-1540 and held the first Christmas mass in North America. Anhaica, the site of the first Christmas, was discovered in Tallahassee by state archaeologists in the 1980s. Part of it is on the very spot where Florida Governor John W. Martin built his home in the 1930s and named it Anhaica!

Apalachee: Arrowheads and the de Soto Site

In 1539, Native American weapons like the bow and arrow used wood and stone technology. The Spanish wore metal chain link armor and carried crossbows made of metal. The Spanish thought they were protected from Native American's weapons; however, while the stone points of arrowheads shattered on impact with the metal chain links, the bow shaft would still go through the armor. Future Spanish expeditions used a different kind of armor.

Glass beads, metal crossbow tips and chain link armor are artifacts unique to the expedition of Hernando de Soto. Archaeologists uncovered these at the site of Anhaica village in Tallahassee.

Photo courtesy of State of Florida

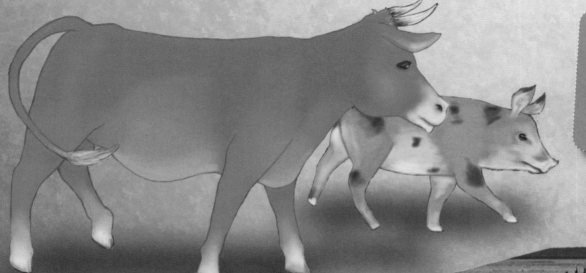

Spanish explorers introduced pigs and cattle to America. So Florida farming has a lot for which to say ¡Gracias!

Mission San Luis

Exploring the site of Mission San Luis made us feel like we were in the 1700s! This recreated mission village is where Spanish missionaries and Apalachee Indians lived side-by-side for almost 50 years. There is a council house covered entirely with thatched palmetto, and living history interpreters show visitors how life was in Tallahassee over 300 years ago!

St. Marks

About 20 miles south of Tallahassee is St. Marks. This small town has a long history of explorers and warriors. Spanish explorer Pánfilo Nárvaez traveled through here in 1528. St. Marks is known today for its abundant stone crab and unspoiled natural beauty. Each fall, St. Marks is also a rest stop for monarch butterflies on their migratory route to Mexico.

Photo courtesy of St. Marks National Wildlife Refuge

Preserving Florida's History!

We couldn't stop saying "wow!" at the Museum of Florida History! This museum has many carefully preserved objects and interactive exhibits that tell the story of Florida's unique history, people, environment and art from thousands of years ago. We encountered an enormous ancient mastodon skeleton named Herman, and saw neat antique cars people used when they visited Florida in the old days. At this museum we learned so much about Florida's history and the importance of preserving it.

Photo courtesy of State of Florida

The R. A. Gray Building in Tallahassee was specifically designed to be a home for the Department of State's archaeological conservation lab, Museum of Florida History, and State Library and Archives of Florida.

The *Science* of Florida History?!

Objects from Florida's past (called artifacts) have been discovered all over the state. Some of the artifacts on display in the museum are from shipwrecks discovered under the ocean. Salty sea water can be damaging and make the artifacts unstable and fall apart. Scientists in the Department of State's conservation lab treat artifacts from under the ocean through a process called electrolysis, where salt from ocean water is taken out of metal objects. Sometimes it can take years to stabilize these amazing artifacts for museum displays.

Herman's bones were found in the fresh water of Wakulla Springs, which is near Tallahassee. Museum staff assembled the skeleton as one of its first exhibits in 1977.

Photo courtesy of Visit Tallahassee

Ally and Jordi's Exploring Experiment:

How Salt is Made

If you have ever been swimming in the ocean, then you probably noticed how salty the water can be. Salt is a mineral that is found naturally in the sea. We took a small cup of seawater and left it in a sunny spot for about a week. We made sure nothing got inside but didn't cover it up. Pretty soon only shiny, brittle salt crystals were left in the cup! You can try it too!

Florida Natural Areas Inventory (FNAI)

Biologists and naturalists have studied Florida's diverse ecosystems for hundreds of years. Today scientists at the Florida Natural Areas Inventory record the plants and environment that make up Florida's natural communities. The saltmarsh, like the one at St. Marks, is one of those special environments.

Tampa: A Real Treasure

This coastal city has some real gems - and not just the ones hidden by Gaspar the Pirate! Gaspar is so legendary that Tampa has the *Gasparilla Festival* every year! Other treasures here include a zoo, vibrant historic districts and the oldest Spanish restaurant in the U.S.

¡Viva La (Industrial) Revolution!

One of Florida's most successful industries is aerospace engineering. Did you know the first commercial flight EVER took off from St. Petersburg and landed in Tampa just 23 minutes later? That was on January 1, 1914, and was aboard a flying boat! We've come a long way since then. Today, Florida has the most licensed seaplane pilots in the entire country.

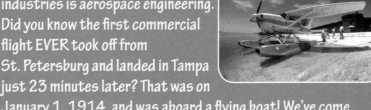

Tampa has been major league baseball's spring training home since the Grapefruit League started in the 1920s.

Tampa: A World Trading Hub

All kinds of industries came to Tampa after Henry Plant brought the railroad. Suddenly, it was possible to move goods around the world faster than ever before. With the railroad, the deep water port and steamships, the possibility of trading from central Florida opened new possibilities for Florida industries.

Tampa Bay Hotel

Henry Plant opened this place as a five-story resort in 1891. It was designed with unique features, like six golden towers, called minarets Henry Plant owned the Plant System of railroads that brought guests to the west coast of Florida. He had a competition with Henry Flagler, who owned another railway line and built resort hotels on the east coast. Their friendly rivalry opened up the state for tourism and laid the foundation for Florida's future success.

A Blue Ribbon Affair

The Florida State Fair is held in Tampa for 12 days each year. It is the official state fair. Florida residents create exhibits about their agricultural businesses — everything from flowers, woodcarving and crafts, to seafood, cattle and pigs. Not to mention all the yummy food.

Polly Parker

Key Forts in Tampa Bay

In the clear waters of Tampa Bay, there are a few small islands called keys. In the 1800s, the U.S. Army built fort defenses in this area; Fort DeSoto on Mullet Key and Fort Dade on Egmont Key.

Fort DeSoto

Egmont Key

This key was used by the U.S. military in 1858, at the end of the Third Seminole War when many Seminole Indians were gathered here before traveling to Oklahoma on the steamship *Grey Cloud*. It was a sad time in history, but there's a happy story of a Seminole woman named Polly Parker. When *Grey Cloud* stopped at St. Marks near Tallahassee, she escaped and ran to freedom until she made it home to Okeechobee. That's over 300 miles! Many of the Seminole Tribe of Florida's most revered medicine people and leaders are Polly's great-grandchildren.

Fort DeSoto

Named after the Spanish explorer Hernando de Soto who landed in the area in 1539, Fort DeSoto Park is a county park with plenty to explore. There are beaches, hiking trails and old artillery batteries from the Spanish-American War. There are also lots of nesting birds to watch. We visited the park and caught the ferry to Egmont Key.

Ybor City

When the port of Tampa became an international port, many workers from Cuba, Germany, Italy and Spain came to the area and created vibrant neighborhoods like Ybor City. The remnants from that early multicultural city can be seen today in the Ybor City Historic District, which is listed on the National Register of Historic Places.

Sarasota

Sarasota is a city located 60 miles south of Tampa. Its most famous former resident was John Ringling, who was one of the masterminds behind the Ringling Bros. and Barnum and Bailey Circus. John's brother Charles was the other. This world-famous show, called *The Greatest Show on Earth*, amazed crowds for 146 years. John and Mable Ringling built a mansion in Sarasota that is now a museum where we learned more about the circus and saw some very famous art.

Ca'd'zan was John and Mable Ringling's Florida mansion. Today it is part of the Ringling Art Museum.

Acrobatic Performers

The tradition of circus performing is often passed down through families. A very famous performing family of acrobats are from Sarasota; they're called The Flying Wallendas. For seven generations, this family has performed high wire stunts, like human pyramids on tightropes without safety harnesses! Nik Wallenda was the first person to walk across Niagara Falls on a tightrope, and in 2013 he walked across the Grand Canyon without a safety harness or a net!

Dolly Jacobs

Another performer from Sarasota is the aerialist legend, Dolly Jacobs. She has been recognized for her art with several awards and accolades, including the title of National Heritage Fellow. She is also from a talented circus family, and has been performing in the circus since she was 16 years old!

Daytona

In case the excitement of the circus wasn't enough, the Daytona area is another great place for thrills. The "Birthplace of Speed" in Ormond Beach, sits just north of Daytona, where today car and motorcycle enthusiasts come to enjoy the exhilarating sport of motor racing.

Mary McLeod Bethune

Mary McLeod Bethune (1875–1955) was an advocate for the advancement of women and African-Americans. As a child, Bethune wondered why the white children of her mother's employer could read, while her African-American friends could not. This inspired her to become a teacher and a Civil Rights leader. In 1904, she established the school in Daytona that became Bethune-Cookman University. She was a very wise woman who advised several presidents on African-American affairs and was appointed to represent the U.S. at the United Nations in 1945.

Aerodynamic Leaders in Florida
Embry-Riddle Aeronautical University was founded soon after the first commercial flight in Tampa. It is one of the most unique universities in the world, teaching aerospace, technology and engineering as well as flying. We visited for one of their week-long summer camps, where we learned amazing things about science and technology!

The Space Coast
From Daytona in the north to Cape Canaveral in the south, the east central coast of Florida is called the Space Coast. The National Aeronautics and Space Administration — known as NASA — has been at Cape Canaveral since 1962, and in 1970, Embry-Riddle Aeronautical University moved to Daytona Beach. Florida's Space Coast is a center for excellence in science, technology, engineering and mathematics (STEM).

We choose to go to the Moon.
After President John F. Kennedy announced his determination to send man to the moon, NASA was established at Cape Canaveral. It was here that Apollo 11 launched on July 16, 1969. Four days later, television viewers around the world were inspired as they watched Neil Armstrong take the first steps on the moon. Today, many businesses dedicated to exploring space are headquartered in Florida. We were inspired to attend Space Camp, where we learned what it takes to be an astronaut and travel to space!

Orlando

Because Florida is the place where dreams come true, sometimes we have to pinch each other to make sure we're not dreaming! Especially when we visit Orlando. Walt Disney chose Orlando for his larger-than-life theme park. Now Orlando has many theme parks and is one of the top ten destinations in the U.S.

Tourism is one of Florida's top industries!

Orange you glad you came to Florida?

Nothing says Florida better than a juicy sweet orange. Oranges have been a part of Florida since Spanish explorers brought them here in the 1500s. There are many different kinds of Florida oranges, thanks to the pioneering cross-pollination work of Lue Gim Gong (ca. 1860 – 1925). He created citrus varieties that could withstand frosty winters. Today, there are more than 8,000 Florida orange growers contributing to this multibillion-dollar Florida industry.

Florida Wildlife Corridor

We love Florida's natural treasures, and Florida's environmentally sensitive lands have been protected since the 1850s. In the central Florida area today, there are millions of acres of conservation land providing habitat for endangered and threatened species. The idea of the corridor is to protect a statewide network of lands and water, sort of like an animal super highway. That way animals can access their natural range of territory.

When Disney came to Florida

In the 1960s, cartoon entrepreneur Walt Disney, came to Florida to find the best place to build a new kind of tourist attraction – a theme park dedicated to his characters. Florida was a popular tourist attraction already (thanks to the two Henrys - Flagler and Plant), and Orlando seemed like the perfect place for the fantasy world where visitors are greeted by characters they could only imagine. We think Orlando was the perfect spot too, and so do over 60 million tourists who visit the city every year.

Ally and Jordi love looking up at the stars.

Can you help them find their way around the constellations?

Start

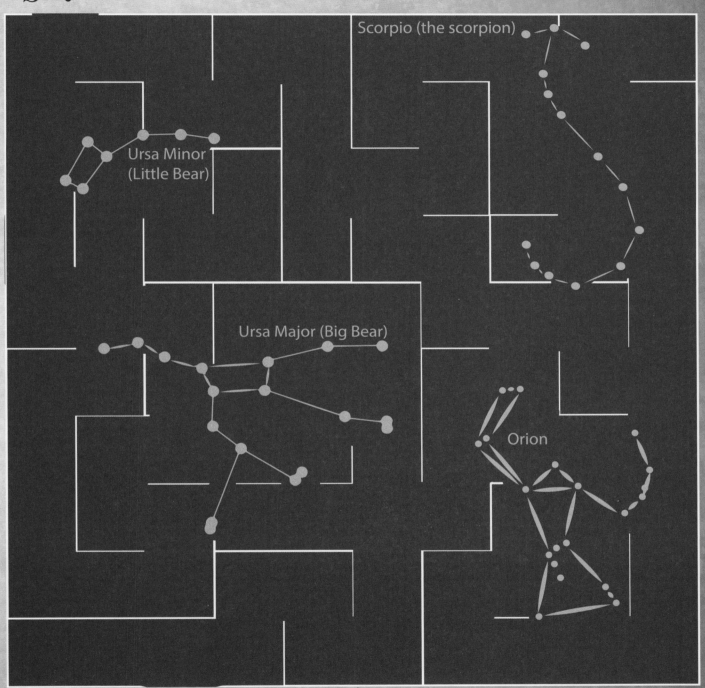

Scorpio (the scorpion)

Ursa Minor
(Little Bear)

Ursa Major (Big Bear)

Orion

Finish

The Treasure Coast

This area gets its glitzy name from the Spanish treasure fleet shipwrecks of 1715. Much of the treasure was recovered from ships at the time, but some was lost forever. Today, the coasts of Indian River, St. Lucie, Martin and Palm Beach counties share the treasure of art, history and rich cultural diversity.

The Highwaymen

Along Florida's east coast during the 1960s, travelers on U.S. Route 1 could buy colorful paintings from young African-American artists who are now known as the Highwaymen. Today you can visit the Highwaymen Heritage Trail in Fort Pierce and see their bright images of Florida scenes.

There are 25 Highwaymen inducted into the Florida Artist's Hall of Fame, and there is also a Highwaywoman! Her name is Mary Ann Carroll.

Highwayman R. L. Lewis

Vero Man

In 1915, Dr. Elias Sellards investigated the discovery of ancient human and animal fossils uncovered while a crew was digging the Vero Canal in the town of Vero Beach. The fossilized bones were from mastodon and other long-extinct animals and were the same age as the fossilized remains of "Vero Man." The discovery was the first in America to prove that people lived at the same time as now extinct animals. Before 1915, no one believed that people lived in Florida 10,000 years ago. We now know that people lived in Florida as early as 14,000 years ago!

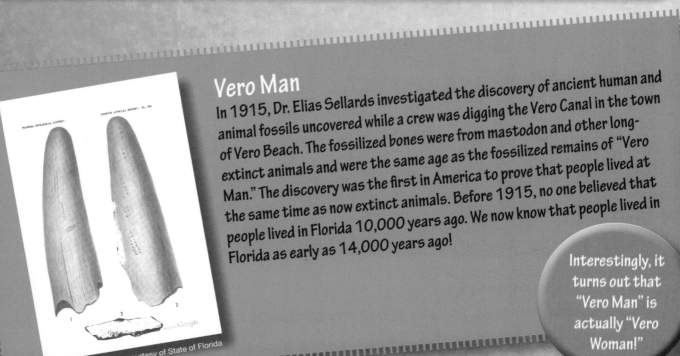
Photo courtesy of State of Florida

Interestingly, it turns out that "Vero Man" is actually "Vero Woman!"

Domo, Yamoto (Colony): Morikami Museum and Gardens

We got a taste of far-east culture right here in Delray Beach at the Morikami Museum and Gardens. This site was once a farming colony called Yamoto, which was developed by Japanese settlers in 1904. Thanks to the park's founder George Morikami, it is now a preserved haven of Japanese culture and beauty with many cultivated Japanese plants. Today, you can visit the old Yamoto colony and learn about Japanese culture through the museum, architecture, food and cultural programming.

Photo courtesy of State of Florida

Fort Lauderdale

Florida's Boating Capital of the World

Fort Lauderdale on Florida's east coast is a magnet for fun in the sun. The charm of the Atlantic Ocean pulled us onto one of the many boats moored in this city and rolled us out on the deep blue waves. After our day out on a charter cruise, we discovered the "lure" of Fort Lauderdale comes from being the boating capital of the world in the state that is the fishing capital of the world. It's a perfect combination!

Miami

This glamourous metropolis is surrounded by water – the Miami River, Biscayne Bay and the Atlantic Ocean are as much a part of the city as the lively art, people and culture.

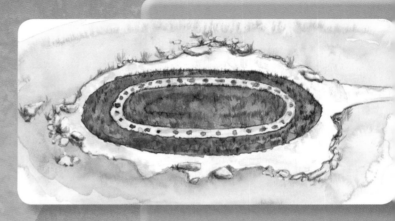

It's a Jungle out there!

It's no surprise that Miami is one of the most popular tourist destinations in the world. There are so many amazing things to see and do here! Our favorite is visiting the unusual theme parks with exotic animals living in jungle-like environments. Parrots, monkeys, big cats and more live on island-like settings around the Miami metropolis.

The Tequesta

We visited a park where an ancient circular building foundation built by Native Americans, possibly the Tequesta Indians, is preserved underground. It is called the Miami Circle.

Early Spanish explorers recorded the name of the Tequesta Indians. The Tequesta and their ancestors crafted wooden dugout canoes that they used to catch deep-sea fish, like shark.

Pineapple, Mango and Guava, oh my!

Lots of people think only citrus and strawberries are grown in Florida, but did you know that pineapple was a major Florida crop in the 1800s? The tropical climate of South Florida makes it one of the best places in the country to grow delicious tropical fruit varieties like mango, lychee, starfruit and avocado. Today there are more than 10,000 delicious acres of tropical fruit farmland in the Miami area, worth about $78 million each year.

Vizcaya

We were so enchanted by this amazing villa overlooking Biscayne Bay that we just had to go inside! Built by American industrialist James Deering in 1914, Vizcaya Museum and Gardens was once his winter home. We saw hand-picked art and artifacts that were collected on travels through Europe, especially Italy. The house and gardens next to the water are a peaceful escape from busy downtown Miami.

The Road to Freedom

In the 1960s many Cubans immigrated to Miami seeking freedom from Cuban dictator Fidel Castro. They first came to the ornate Miami News building, which became a symbol of Cuban-American freedom. It is known today as the Freedom Tower.

Get on Your Feet!

One Cuban family who made a new life in Miami was the Fajardo family. Their eldest daughter, Gloria, married another Cuban-American, Emilio Estefan, and became a famous singer and songwriter. Their band was called "The Miami Sound Machine." Gloria later co-authored the musical named after one of her famous songs, "Get on your feet!" In 2013, she was inducted into the Florida Artists Hall of Fame, and in 2015 both Gloria Estefan and her husband, Emilio, received the Presidential Medal of Freedom.

Photo courtesy of World Red Eye

Gloria and Emilio Estefan

Miami is truly a multicultural city and is often called the capital of Latin America.

Virginia Key Beach

Just south of Miami Beach is a barrier island called Virginia Key, where we played for hours on the sandy beach and even toured a major aquatic theme park. Virginia Key was a segregated beach at one time. Today, all are welcome at this historic City of Miami coastal park.

Gateway to the Americas

Miami is known as the Cruise Capital of The World with nearly 5 million cruise passengers traveling through the Port of Miami each year. Access to the waterways is big for business, too. The Port of Miami supports more than 200,000 jobs in the region and enables international trade networks that span the entire world.

Florida Keys

South of Miami, there are hundreds of little islands called keys. Some of them are connected by the Overseas Highway. Visiting the Florida Keys is like taking a Caribbean getaway that's still close to home. In fact, the Keys have been popular with settlers from the Bahamas for hundreds of years. You can really tell from the style of houses and laid back lifestyle!

To preserve the ocean and its beauty, Florida's underwater tour guides remind everybody: take only pictures and leave only bubbles!

Exploring Underwater in South Florida

There is so much water and natural beauty in and around Florida, it is no wonder that our state is home to America's first underwater state park - John Pennekamp Coral Reef State Park! We got to go snorkeling here in the clear blue ocean. On our underwater adventures we saw a statue in the water called "Christ of the Abyss." All kinds of colorful fish danced around it!

Florida Underwater Preserves

Near Indian Key, we dove around the San Pedro underwater shipwreck preserve. We saw vibrant fish darting around the shipwreck and a sea turtle using the replica cannon to scratch its back! The San Pedro was one of the Spanish galleon fleet that sank during a hurricane in 1733. With 12 underwater shipwreck preserves in Florida, there is plenty to explore below the surface!

Key Westerners affectionately call themselves Conche and the island The Conch Republic!

The Keys, By the Numbers

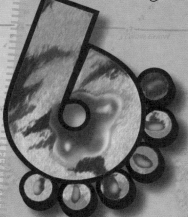

6 Toed Cats

Key West has been called home by some famous people, like Ernest Hemingway, the Nobel Prize-winning author of the books "A Farewell to Arms" and "The Old Man and the Sea." While living in Key West, he was given a white polydactyl cat – a cat with six toes on each paw. Today many polydactyl cats live at the Ernest Hemingway Home and Museum. They are descendants of that original cat.

President Harry S. Truman is another famous Key West figure. He had a winter home near today's Naval Air Station Key West, which he called his "Little White House."

7 Islands of the Dry Tortugas National Park

There are seven islands near Key West that make up the Dry Tortugas National Park. The name comes from Juan Ponce de León's records from 1513; he called the islands "Las Tortugas" (meaning The Turtles). And for good reason. There are a lot of turtles who lay their eggs here!

List of Seven Keys of the Dry Tortugas:
Bush Key
East Key
Garden Key
Hospital Key
Loggerhead Key
Long Key
Middle Key

Garden Key is one of the seven islands. It is the site of a huge brick fortress called Fort Jefferson. Fort Jefferson was built just before the Civil War and was also used as a prison. After President Abraham Lincoln died on April 15, 1865, Dr. Samuel Mudd was imprisoned on Fort Jefferson. Dr. Mudd was accused of being an accomplice by helping John Wilkes Booth escape after Booth shot the President.

8th Wonder of the World!

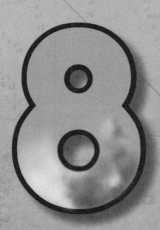

Key West is the last island in The Keys. Before 1912, the only access to Key West was by boat. This changed when Henry Flagler built a railroad across the ocean, connecting the islands. This amazing engineering feat was called the eighth wonder of the world at the time. Sadly, the track was badly damaged in the 1935 Labor Day hurricane and could no longer be used. Instead of repairing it, part of the structure was reused to create the Overseas Highway, which is still in use today.

Fort Myers

This city sits close to the coast of the Gulf of Mexico at the mouth of the Caloosahatchee River. There were some very early residents, known as the Calusa, who lived in this area when Spanish explorers arrived. The current city was incorporated in 1885.

 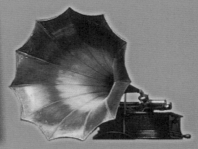 

Good Friends and Great Ideas

We visited the Edison & Ford Winter Estates and were blown away by Thomas Edison's amazing inventions on display in his old laboratory! He invented the lightbulb, the phonograph (a sound recording machine), and the first moving-image camera. Edison's winter home was just a stone's throw away from his Ford motorcar inventing friend, Henry Ford's house. These two friends probably shared many ideas that shaped our future.

DID YOU KNOW?
Lake Okeechobee is the 4th largest freshwater lake wholly in the U.S.!

Lake Okeechobee

Canals have been built around Lake Okeechobee for over a thousand years! Today a system of canals and locks control the water flow of Lake Okeechobee and the surrounding farmland. Yummy sweet sugarcane, vegetable crops and even pretty flowers are grown in this area. There are also acres of cattle ranches.

Sometimes, dugout canoes are exposed when water levels go down during Florida's dry season. If you find one, it's important to call an archaeologist who will know what to do.

Calusa Indians – People of the Water

The Calusa were a southwest Florida tribe of Native Americans who lived atop huge shell mounds when Spanish explorers arrived in the 1500s. In some coastal areas, shell mounds towered so high they became islands, like Mound Key in Estero Bay. These mounds are recognized as a unique Florida upland coastal ecosystem. They are characterized by shell deposits made by ancient Native Americans, mangroves and tropical trees, such as the Strangler Fig (or Banyan Tree) and Gumbo Limbo.

Florida is the fishing capital of the world and Lake Okeechobee is one of the best places in South Florida to catch freshwater fish. The lake covers 730 square miles and is full of Largemouth Bass, Speckled Perch and Bluegill.

The People of the Water

We took a canoe ride, and our guide told us this story: Once upon a time, the People of the Water lived in villages around Lake Okeechobee. Some villages, like the one at Fort Center, were big cities with canals running through them. The people built sturdy dugout canoes to travel great distances for trade.

Naples

We love coming to Naples – it is just like coming home! There are beaches, museums and libraries. There is also amazing wilderness to explore, including the National Panther Wildlife Refuge, Big Cypress, and Ten Thousand Islands National Wildlife Refuge.

C'MON – Let's Go!

Our love of exploration began when we visited the Children's Museum of Naples (C'MON). Kids can play, learn and explore with their families at this fun-filled museum. We explored the seasons, science, art and even found out what it was like to be a train conductor! The library was our favorite part, where our imaginations explored beyond Florida!

Ted Smallwood's Store

One of the most off-the-beaten-track museums we have ever been to is the Historic Smallwood Store. It was founded in 1906 on a small island south of Naples. Originally, it was a trading post where pioneer settlers traded furs, bought supplies and received their mail. It became an important resource also for the Seminole and Miccosukee people living in the area. Today, it is a museum where we learned how pioneers adapted to live in this remote place.

All SeaBoard!

We shared even more train fun at the Naples Depot and Train Museum. These two museums are in the restored 1926 historic Seaboard Coast Line Railway station. We rode the miniature train along Tenth Street and Fifth Avenue. Inside we saw detailed miniature towns come to life!

Everglades

Florida Everglades National Park covers 2,538 square miles on the southwest tip of Florida. We took an airboat tour to see this breathtaking UNESCO World Heritage Site. Although many tourists like us visit, it is the native land of The Seminole Tribe of Florida and the Miccosukee Indians of Florida, who call the Everglades Pa-hay-okee, meaning Grassy Water, or River of Grass.

Marjorie Stoneman Douglas (1890 – 1998)
In her book, *Everglades: River of Grass*, Marjorie Stoneman Douglas wrote, "There are no other Everglades in the world." She brought attention to this special part of Florida and was called the Mother of the Everglades because of her conservation work. She was central to the formation of Everglades National Park and the protection of its delicate aquatic ecosystems.

UNESCO stands for United Nations Educational, Scientific and Cultural Organization. It is part of the United Nations.

Nature
The shallow grassy water of the Everglades seems to go on forever, but there are actually several distinct ecosystems supporting endangered plants and animals like the Florida Panther. There are mangrove forests along the Gulf of Mexico coast, and sawgrass with palm and cypress tree hammocks inland. Everglades National Park is the largest mangrove and sawgrass ecosystem in the western hemisphere, and the most important breeding ground for wading birds in North America.

Florida Panther

Ally and Jordi Find It Fun!

Throughout our journey, we saw a lot of interesting things! Here's a closer look at some of the things we saw. Do you remember seeing these things too? Can you find them in the book?

State Butterfly: Zebra Longwing
Long black wings with thin yellow bands, combined with slow, graceful flight, characterize the Zebra Longwing. It has a wide range of habitats, including hardwood hammocks, thickets, and gardens. In 1996, the state legislature designated the Zebra Longwing as the official state butterfly.

The French in Florida
When the French ruled Florida in 1565, they used a different flag. It was blue with three golden designs called fleurs-de-lis. After the French Revolution in 1789, the French changed the design to the flag we know today; three equal vertical stripes of blue, white and red.

State Wildflower: Coreopsis
The flower of the genus Coreopsis was designated as Florida's official wildflower in 1991, after the colorful flowers were used extensively in Florida's roadside plantings and highway beautification programs. The coreopsis is found in a variety of colors, ranging from golden to pink.

The Florida Cracker Horse
The Florida Cracker Horse is descended from early Spanish breeds. In 2008, our legislature designated the Florida Cracker Horse as the official state horse.

St. Augustine Lighthouse and Keepers' Quarters
The St. Augustine Lighthouse and Keepers' Quarters were added to the National Register of Historic Places in 1981. The National Register of Historic Places is the official list of our country's historic buildings, districts, sites, structures, and objects worthy of preservation. It was established as part of the National Historic Preservation Act of 1966 and is overseen by the National Park Service.

State Shell: Horse Conch
The horse conch, also known as the giant band shell, has been Florida's official state shell since 1969. This shell is native to the marine waters around Florida and can grow to a length of 24 inches. Young horse conchs have orange-colored shells; adults have orange apertures. The word "conch" comes from a Greek word meaning "shell."

The Great Seal of the State of Florida
The elements and basic design of the first state seal of Florida were established in 1868 and had mountains and a different palm tree. The current state seal was created in 1985, does not have mountains (since Florida doesn't have any mountains) and includes the sabal palmetto palm – Florida's State Tree.

Great Blue Heron
The Great Blue Heron is the largest heron in North America and is a regular sight in Florida's waterways. They are wading birds with blue-gray plumage and a black plume. They often stand motionless in the water, then strike at lightning fast speeds to catch their prey.

State Gem: The Moonstone

United States astronauts Neil Armstrong and Edwin ("Buzz") Aldrin landed on the moon on July 20, 1969 aboard the Apollo 11 spacecraft. Since this and all other astronaut-controlled spaceflights had been launched from the Kennedy Space Center in Brevard County, the Florida legislature sought to memorialize this "giant step" for humankind. In 1970, lawmakers adopted the moonstone as the official state gem.

The National Naval Aviation Museum

The United States Navy's Blue Angels Flight Demonstration Squadron is housed at the National Naval Aviation Museum in Pensacola. The Museum has 350,000 square feet of exhibit space and is home to tens of thousands of items and documents which span the entire spectrum of Naval Aviation's history.

State Fruit/Flower/Beverage: Orange

Oranges are a major part of Florida's economy. The blossom of the orange tree is very fragrant and millions of these white flowers perfume the atmosphere throughout central and south Florida during the spring. The orange blossom was selected as the state flower by the legislature in 1909, and orange juice was designated as the official state beverage in 1967. Oddly enough, it would be years later in 2005, before the orange was recognized as the state fruit.

Sailfish

Sailfish are found nearly everywhere there is warm ocean water. The average size of sailfish found in Florida is approximately six to seven feet and 30 to 45 pounds. The 1975 Florida legislature adopted the Atlantic sailfish as the state's official saltwater fish.

Florida Shrimp and Seafood

Shrimp from Florida are shipped worldwide. Did you know that in one year, more than 19 million pounds of shrimp (worth about $50 million) are caught in Florida's waters? It's the top seafood species caught in Florida.

State Tree: Sabal Palm

The sabal palm is the most widely distributed palm in Florida. It grows in almost any soil and has many uses, including food, medicine and landscaping. The Florida legislature designated the sabal palm as the state tree, and later mandated that the sabal palm replace the cocoa palm on the state seal.

Sunshine Skyway Bridge

The Sunshine Skyway Bridge in Tampa was opened in 1987 and is the longest cable-stayed concrete bridge in the world. The bridge is 190 feet above the water, and is 29,040 feet long; that's more than four miles! The bridge has two towers, each with 21 steel cables that extend in either direction from the towers to hold the bridge up. More than 50,000 cars cross the bridge every day.

State Reptile: American Alligator

In 1987, the Florida legislature designated the American alligator as the official state reptile. The alligator originally symbolized Florida's extensive untamed wilderness and swamps. Alligators are found throughout Florida and in parts of other southeastern states. They prefer lakes, swamps, canals, and other wetland habitats.

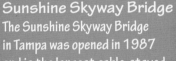

ca. 12,000 B.C.

People first moved into Florida at the end of the last Ice Age.

5,000 B.C.

Florida's first people established the first permanent settlements, primarily on the coast.

1513

Spanish explorer Juan Ponce de León arrived on the east coast of the land he named La Florida. In 152 he returned but was fatally wound by the Calusa.

1738

Fort Mose, north of St. Augustine, became the first legally-sanctioned free black community in what is now the United States.

1763

After the Seven Years' War, England acquired Florida and divided it into East and West Florida.

1783

Spain resumed control of Florida.

1835

The Second Seminole War began and continued until 1842.

1845

On March 3, Florida was approved for statehood.

1855-58

The Third Seminole War was fought

1891

Developer Henry Plant opened the Tampa Bay Hotel.

1898

The Spanish-American War saw embarkation camps at Tampa, Miami and Jacksonville.

1903

The history of automotive competition in Daytona Beach began with a friendly contest between two gentlemen debatin who had the fastest early automobile. The first race was at Ormond Beach, which is called the "Birthplace of Speed"

Florida's History

1539

ernando de Soto's expedition ntroduced pigs to Florida and held e first North American Christmas Anhaica (modern day Tallahassee.)

1564

French explorers came to Florida and established Fort Caroline in present day Jacksonville.

1565

Pedro Menéndez de Avilés established St. Augustine, the first permanent European settlement in North America. With his arrival came the first citrus trees to Florida. Today, the Sunshine State produces almost three-quarters of the nation's oranges.

1818

Andrew Jackson invaded Florida, during the First Seminole War.

1821

Through the Adams-Onís Treaty, Florida became a U.S. territory, with Andrew Jackson as the first governor.

1824

Tallahassee was established as the Florida capital, and the first Capitol building was a log cabin.

1861

he Civil War began and continued rough 1865. The Battle of Olustee nd the Battle of Natural Bridge were wo incidents that further shaped lorida's future.

1885

A new state constitution was adopted, replacing the 1868 version.

1888

Railroad baron Henry Flagler completed the Ponce de León Hotel in St. Augustine.

1961

On May 5, Alan Shepard, the first American astronaut, was launched into space from Cape Canaveral Space Center (later called Cape Kennedy).

1971

Walt Disney World opened in Orlando.

1985

A new state seal was created to correct inaccuracies dating to 1868.

Puzzle Solutions

Puzzle solution: page 17

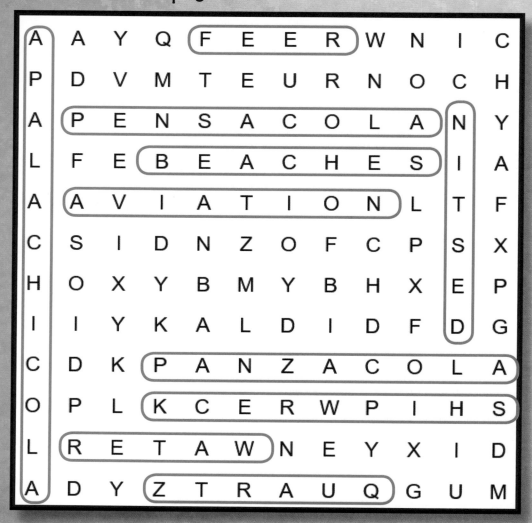

Puzzle solution: page 23

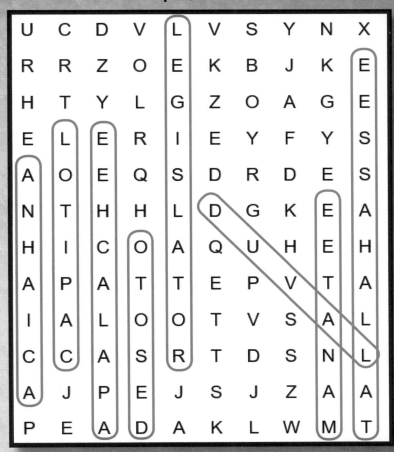

Puzzle solution: page 33

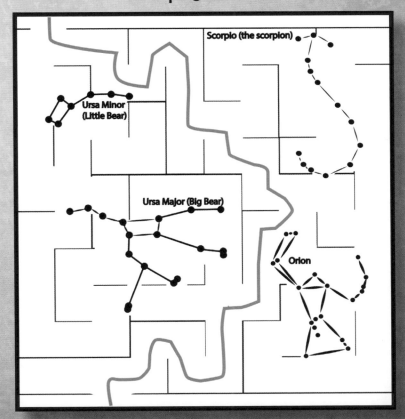

Dedication

This book is dedicated to all the children of Florida. Reading books allows children, and adults alike, to travel away to wonderful places and experience fascinating things. Reading books also stimulates growth and learning. Children who read independently score higher on achievement tests in all subject areas and enjoy academic success.

My hope is that this book will encourage children to explore all of the wonderful history, nature, places and opportunities that Florida has to offer. We know that through the act of reading, children can have a hand in shaping their own destiny. Remember, great readers become great leaders!

Resources

Find links to teacher resources
on our website at:
allyandjordisadventures.com

Students:
Find more fun things to do
on our website at:
allyandjordisadventures.com